W9-BWG-315

ALTERNATOR BOOKS™

WHO INVENTED THE
MOVIE CAMERA?

EDISON VS. FRIESE-GREENE

Karen Latchana Kenney

Lerner Publications ◆ Minneapolis

Lerner Publications Company
A division of Lerner Publishing Group, Inc.
241 First Avenue North
Minneapolis, MN 55401 USA

For reading levels and more information, look up this title at www.lernerbooks.com.

Main body text set in Aptifer Slab Regular 11.5/18.
Typeface provided by Linotype AG.

Library of Congress Cataloging-in-Publication Data

Names: Kenney, Karen Latchana, author.
Title: Who invented the movie camera? : Edison vs. Friese-Greene / by Karen Latchana Kenney.
Description: Minneapolis : Lerner Publications, [2018] | Series: STEM smackdown | Audience: Age 8–12. | Audience: Grades 4 to 6. | Includes bibliographical references and index.
Identifiers: LCCN 2017029267| ISBN 9781512483239 (library bound) | ISBN 9781541512085 (paperback) | ISBN 9781512483260 (eBook PDF)
Subjects: LCSH: Motion picture cameras—History—Juvenile literature. | Edison, Thomas A. (Thomas Alva), 1847–1931—Juvenile literature. | Friese-Greene, William, 1855–1921—Juvenile literature.
Classification: LCC TR880 .K46 2018 | DDC 777—dc23

LC record available at https://lccn.loc.gov/2017029267

Manufactured in the United States of America
1-43336-33156-10/2/2017

CONTENTS

FIRST FILMMAKERS

The theater lights dim, and the crowd hushes. The newest sci-fi thriller is about to start. You slide on your 3-D glasses and wait for this epic movie to begin. Soon you're whisked away to another world where aliens battle humans. Spaceships soar through the stars and seem to come right at you. Laser sounds boom from speakers all around you. Are you ready for this intergalactic voyage?

Movies have come a long way since movie cameras were invented more than a century ago.

A modern movie camera

Movies make pictures come to life. They create worlds you can escape into. But just a little more than a century ago, the art of making pictures move was out of reach. The race to become the mastermind behind the movie camera took off in 1870, with the invention of film that could be **exposed** in a fraction of a second, rather than the hour needed at the dawn of photography. After that first hurdle was cleared, inventors started focusing on a camera that could take pictures rapidly, one after the other. Projecting them quickly would give the illusion of motion on a screen.

Two contenders squared off. One was the already well-known American inventor Thomas Edison. The other wasn't quite as famous—British photographer William Friese-Greene. These two filmmakers on opposite sides of the Atlantic would compete to make moving pictures a reality. Who would be the front-running filmmaker?

5

CHAPTER 1

TELEGRAPHER TURNED INVENTOR

In 1847, when Thomas Edison was born in Milan, Ohio, the **telegraph** was *the* way to communicate. This invention would lead young Thomas to his life as an inventor. At the age of thirteen, Thomas took his first job selling newspapers, magazines, and candy on the Grand Trunk Railroad. This is when he began seriously studying the telegraph.

By the age of fifteen, Thomas was a telegraph operator for the railroad. From 1863 to 1868, he traveled from city to city to work. He learned all he could about electrical science and technology and began to invent. In 1867 he made a device that allowed him to record telegraph messages more accurately. It was the first of Thomas's many inventions.

Thomas sold candy and newspapers to railroad passengers. Meanwhile, in the baggage car of the train, he set up a chemical laboratory to perform experiments and a small printing press where he made his own newspapers.

Edison's first big invention was a machine that could record and play back sound. The financial stability and name recognition he gained from this win helped set him up for success as he started work on his next inventions.

ENTERING THE BIG LEAGUES

In 1869 Edison settled in New York City. The city was the perfect training ground for the rising superstar. He soon had contracts for his telegraph inventions, and in 1876, he opened his laboratory at Menlo Park, New Jersey.

Edison stepped up to the big leagues in November 1877 with his invention of the **phonograph**, the first machine that could record and play back sound. He kept inventing with continued success.

Eadweard Muybridge (*pictured*) was an experienced photographer when he became fascinated with moving pictures. He inspired Edison to combine moving images with the phonograph.

British photographer Eadweard Muybridge became interested in Edison's phonograph. Muybridge visited Edison in February 1888 with an idea: What if they could find a way to pair the phonograph's sound with a series of photographs? That would make talking moving pictures.

Edison took on this challenge, writing in October: "I am experimenting upon an instrument which does for the eye what the phonograph does for the ear, which is the recording and reproduction of things in motion." Edison was on his way to creating a movie camera. But he didn't realize that someone else was already in the motion picture game.

ASSIST

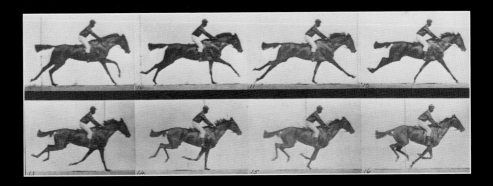

Eadweard Muybridge was interested in animal movement. During the 1870s, he developed a fast camera shutter to take many pictures in a row that would capture a horse's motion (*above*). Muybridge demonstrated his findings about motion in lectures. He showed his photographs on a lantern he had created. His zoopraxiscope projected drawn copies of his pictures quickly one after another onto a screen. This created the illusion of moving pictures.

CHAPTER 2
THE VISIONARY PHOTOGRAPHER

The other heavy hitter hoping to bring moving pictures to life was British photographer William Friese-Greene. Born in Bristol, England, in 1855, William developed an interest in chemistry and physics at a young age. When he was fourteen, he entered the world of photography as an apprentice to a photographer. During the next several years, William learned all he could—from mixing chemical solutions to developing the **glass plates** used to take pictures.

Glass plates (*pictured*) were coated in chemicals and exposed to light in a camera. The negative image appeared on the glass after the plates were developed.

Friese-Greene (*above*) had a background in portrait photography before he began work with the movie camera.

Around 1874 Friese-Greene struck out on his own, opening a photography studio in Bath, England. He was talented at taking portraits and soon opened another studio. Friese-Greene was on his way to becoming a very successful portrait photographer.

Slides from a magic lantern, the machine that was the fore-runner of the movie projector

SEEING MAGIC LANTERNS

When Friese-Greene met John Rudge in 1880, life threw the photographer a curve ball. Rudge had been working on a magic lantern. These machines illuminated single glass slides and projected their images. Rudge made a new lantern called the Biophantascope, which held seven slides on a rotating disk. Each slide showed a stage of movement, and when the machine rotated, it created the illusion of a moving image for a few seconds.

The eye could be tricked into seeing motion if the slides were shown fast enough. Even when a picture is removed from sight, the brain still "sees" it for a fraction of a second. This is called persistence of vision. Showing at least ten images per second would trick the brain into seeing motion.

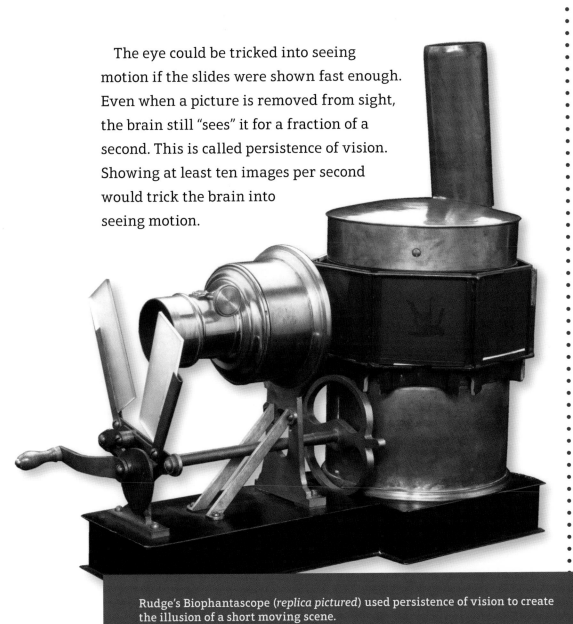

Rudge's Biophantascope (*replica pictured*) used persistence of vision to create the illusion of a short moving scene.

Rudge's Biophantascope sparked Friese-Greene's curiosity: How could he record and show movement? Cameras couldn't take photos that fast then. So Friese-Greene began working on a camera that could. He was ready to go the distance to find the answer.

ASSIST

American inventor George Eastman (*left*) made home photography possible. In 1888 he invented an easy-to-use camera called the Kodak. Inside the camera was a new kind of film that Eastman had invented. The celluloid film was a flexible roll of plastic coated with light-sensitive chemicals. Eastman didn't know it, but his film would become the key to making motion pictures.

George Eastman's Kodak camera (*pictured*) came preloaded with enough celluloid film to take one hundred pictures. When the film was at its end, the user would send the camera back to the factory. There the old film would be developed and a roll of new film would be put into the camera.

A NEW KIND OF FILM

Glass disks, like the one used in Rudge's Biophantascope, were limiting. They only held seven to twelve photographs and could not be moved fast enough to create a realistic appearance of motion. Around 1889 Friese-Greene began experimenting with celluloid film. Because the film was more flexible than glass plates, it could be moved quickly inside a camera. He also experimented with cameras, trying to make one that could take multiple pictures per second.

CHAPTER 3
TAKING THE LEAD

In June 1889, Friese-Greene filed for a **patent** on his movie camera. Inside the camera was a roller with toothed edges. It gripped and quickly pulled a roll of film in front of the shutter to capture an image. The camera could take up to ten pictures per second. He called it a chronophotographic camera.

Friese-Greene had taken the lead in the movie camera race, but Edison would soon pass the front-runner. Earlier that year, Edison had assembled a team to work on a movie camera and viewing device. Scottish inventor William Dickson was the team's leader. He experimented with

Friese-Greene's early movie camera

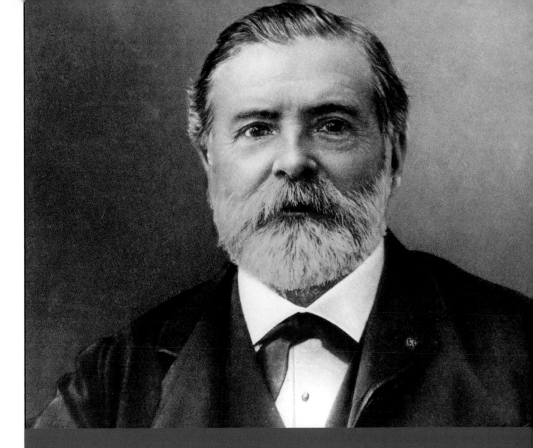
Étienne-Jules Marey (*pictured*) invented a camera that could both take pictures and chart movement. His use of gears helped him take scientific images of his observations.

sheets of celluloid film too. By August the team had made significant progress on the first simple kinetoscope, a machine for viewing movies.

Edison's hot streak continued as he learned about French scientist Étienne-Jules Marey's photographic techniques. His cameras had clockworklike gears. They captured motion by taking precisely timed pictures. Edison used this information to design film in long rolls with **sprocket** holes along the edges.

Edison's sprocket technology remains a key piece of technology in this later version of his kinetoscope movie-viewing device.

Toothed wheels fit into the sprocket holes and pulled the film quickly and precisely through the camera. In 1890 Edison's team began working on the movie camera that the inventor later called the kinetograph.

DROPPING THE BALL

At the same time, Friese-Greene was in trouble. While he was focused on his movie camera, his photography businesses were failing and he was going into debt. If he wanted to stay in the game, he would have to do something fast.

In June 1890, Friese-Greene was invited to speak at the Photographic Convention of the United Kingdom in Chester, England. It was his big break—an opportunity to show the world what he was made of. But on the way to the convention, Friese-Greene's projection machine was damaged. He could not display his films. His camera may have worked, but he wasn't able to publicly show others that it did.

Friese-Greene was in so much debt that he had to serve time in London's Brixton Prison. This image of the prison was taken in 2015.

Looking through the eyepiece at the top of Edison's kinetoscope allowed the viewer to see about twenty seconds of film on a continuous loop.

By 1891 Friese-Greene was **bankrupt**. He had spent too much time inventing instead of managing his portrait studios and owed money to various companies. The promising star was forced to sell the rights of his movie camera patent.

EDISON SPRINTS AHEAD

At the same time, Edison's businesses were thriving, leaving him plenty of funds to invest into his new movie camera and viewer inventions. On August 24, 1891, Edison filed for patents on his movie camera and viewer.

His kinetoscope allowed one person to view a film through a peephole. Inside its large wooden cabinet was a 47-foot-long

HE DID WHAT?

Edison Kinetoscopic Record of a Sneeze Taken Copyright by W.K.L. Dickson Orange NJ — Jan. 7th 94

One of Edison's first films (*left*) shows a simple, everyday action—a sneeze. It was acted out by one of his laboratory workers, Fred Ott, and was filmed on January 7, 1894. The sound of the sneeze was recorded on a phonograph and was played along with the film.

(14 m) strip of film that ran continuously. Edison gave the first public demonstration of the kinetoscope on May 9, 1893, at the Brooklyn Institute of Arts and Sciences in New York. The race appeared to be over—Edison was the champion. He had brought moving pictures to the people.

CHAPTER 4

WHO WAS FIRST?

Edison seemed to be the clear winner in the battle to invent the movie camera, but it was too early to take a victory lap. In 1910 Friese-Greene gave evidence to a US court that he had sent a letter to Edison in June 1889 describing his movie camera in great detail. Friese-Greene had wanted to combine Edison's phonograph with his camera to add sound to his films.

Edison's movie camera was a success! But does he really deserve credit as the champion of the movie camera?

The spooling mechanism of Edison's kinetoscope and film

During the court case, Edison denied receiving Friese-Greene's letter, yet another letter from Friese-Greene was later found in Edison's papers. It referenced the first letter, saying: "Have sent to you by same post a paper with description of Machine Camera for taking 10 [images] a second which may be of interest to you." Was the first letter a game changer for Edison's invention? It *did* come just as Edison was closing in on his kinetograph. Yet it's unlikely that Friese-Greene's letter made much of a difference to Edison's movie camera. Edison's team was already hard at work on their own invention before the letter would have arrived.

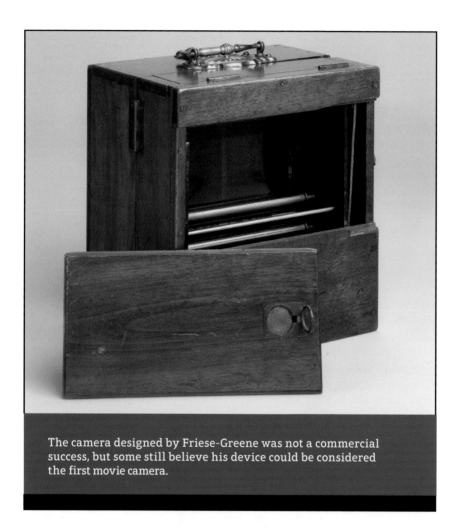

The camera designed by Friese-Greene was not a commercial success, but some still believe his device could be considered the first movie camera.

THE FATHER OF FILM?

Most Americans still claimed Edison was the clear inventor of the movie camera. Yet Friese-Greene's name would continue to make headlines. Some believe his camera (made before Edison's) was the first example of a working movie camera.

In 1948 author Ray Allister wrote a book claiming Friese-Greene was the unknown inventor of the movie camera. She claimed that she had done careful research, yet much of the book contains conversations she imagined Friese-Greene had with other people. Then, in 1951, *The Magic Box*, a film based on Allister's book, came out, continuing to spread Friese-Greene's supposed claim to fame.

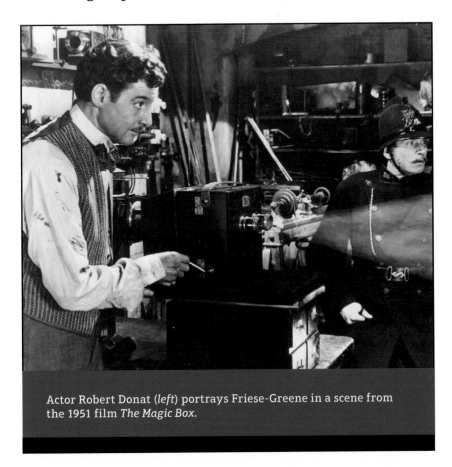

Actor Robert Donat (*left*) portrays Friese-Greene in a scene from the 1951 film *The Magic Box*.

25

Kinetoscope parlors, like this one in San Francisco, started springing up across the country shortly after Edison's success.

Despite Allister's efforts, most people still believe Edison made the first practical movie camera. Friese-Greene played a part in the development of movie cameras and movies, but he was more of a dreamer. He had big ideas, but no money or real mechanical knowledge to create a practical machine. Edison's good business sense kept his invention afloat, and he was able to get working movie cameras and movies to the public first.

THE WINNER!

EDISON

INVENTOR MATCHUP

EDISON

- **POSITION:** Telegrapher/inventor

- **FILING DATE OF FIRST MOVIE CAMERA PATENT:** August 1891

- **TOTAL PATENTS FILED (LIFETIME):** Over 1,000

- **CLAIM TO FAME:** Brought the movie camera and viewer to the public first

VS.

FRIESE-GREENE

- **POSITION:** Photographer

- **FILING DATE OF FIRST MOVIE CAMERA PATENT:** June 1889

- **TOTAL PATENTS FILED (LIFETIME):** Over 70

- **CLAIM TO FAME:** Made a movie camera first

TIMELINE

1880
William Friese-Greene sees John Rudge's Biophantascope and begins working on a camera that can record motion.

1888
Thomas Edison starts working on a machine that can record and reproduce images in motion.

1889
The inventors begin working with celluloid film, and Friese-Greene patents his movie camera.

1890
Friese-Greene fails to demonstrate his film at the Photographic Convention of the United Kingdom because the projector is broken.

SUMMER 1891
Friese-Greene loses his portrait studios and funding for his invention. He declares bankruptcy.

AUGUST 1891
Edison patents his movie camera and viewer.

1893
Edison publicly demonstrates his movies and viewer at the Brooklyn Institute of Arts.

1894
The first kinetoscope parlor (movie theater) opens in New York City.

SOURCE NOTES

8–9 Inventing Entertainment: The Early Motion Pictures and Sound Recordings of the Edison Companies, n.d., Motion Picture, Broadcasting, and Recorded Sound Division, Library of Congress, accessed July 13, 2017, https://www.loc.gov/collections/edison-company-motion-pictures-and-sound-recordings/articles-and-essays/history-of-edison-motion-pictures/.

23 Michael Chanan, *The Dream That Kicks: The Prehistory and Early Years of Cinema in Britain* (London: Routledge, 2005), 67.

GLOSSARY

bankrupt: to not have enough money to be able to pay your bills

celluloid: a flexible substance that is similar to plastic and was used to make motion picture film

exposed: when film is open to light in a camera, which leaves an image on it

glass plates: pieces of glass coated with light-sensitive chemicals to capture images taken in a camera

patent: a legal document giving only an inventor of something the rights to make or sell that invention

phonograph: a machine that plays sounds recorded in the grooves of a record

sprocket: a wheel with a rim made of toothlike points that fit into holes

telegraph: a device for sending messages over long distances using a code of electrical signals sent by wire or radio

FURTHER INFORMATION

Barretta, Gene. *Timeless Thomas: How Thomas Edison Changed Our Lives*. New York: Henry Holt, 2012.

Brasch, Nicolas. *The Industrial Revolution: Age of Invention*. New York: PowerKids, 2014.

"A Brief History of the Movie Camera"—*Popular Mechanics*
http://www.popularmechanics.com/culture/movies/g1046/a-brief-history-of-the-movie-camera/

Hamen, Susan E. *Who Invented the Light Bulb? Edison vs. Swan*. Minneapolis: Lerner Publications, 2018.

Inventing Entertainment: The Early Motion Pictures and Sound Recordings of the Edison Companies—Library of Congress
https://www.loc.gov/collections/edison-company-motion-pictures-and-sound-recordings/about-this-collection/

Motion Pictures—National Park Service
https://www.nps.gov/edis/learn/kidsyouth/motion-pictures.htm

"Persistence of Vision: How Does Animation Work?"—*Future Learn*
https://www.futurelearn.com/courses/explore-animation/0/steps/12222

"Thomas Edison Patented the Kinetoscope"—America's Story
http://www.americaslibrary.gov/jb/gilded/jb_gilded_kinetscp_1.html

INDEX

PHOTO ACKNOWLEDGMENTS

The images in this book are used with the permission of: iStock.com/gyener, p. 1; Mark Agnor/Shutterstock.com, p. 4; iStock.com/guruXOOX, p. 5; Bettmann/Getty Images, pp. 6, 18; Library of Congress (LC-DIG-cwpbh-04044), p. 7; Rischgitz/Hulton Archive/Getty Images, p. 8; Library of Congress (LC-USZ62-52703), p. 9; Tihov Studio/Alamy Stock Photo, p. 10; Science & Society Picture Library/Getty Images, pp. 11, 12, 13, 15, 16, 23, 24, 28 (Friese-Greene); Hulton Archive/Getty Images, p. 14; Stefano Bianchetti/Corbis Historical/Getty Images, p. 17; Dan Kitwood/Getty Images News, p. 19; Universal History Archive/Universal Images Group/Getty Images, p. 20; Library of Congress (LC-DIG-ppmsca-13462), p. 21; Corbis Historical/Getty Images, p. 22; Courtesy Everett Collection, p. 25; Heritage Images/Hulton Archive/Getty Images, p. 26; Library of Congress (LC-USZ62-105139), pp. 27, 28 (Edison); iStock.com/lushik, p. 28 (boxing gloves). Design elements: iStock.com/ivanastar (sunburst background); iStock.com/Allevinatis (boxer body); iStock.com/subtropica (border texture).

Front cover: iStock.com/gyener (movie camera); Science & Society Picture Library/Getty Images (Friese-Greene); Library of Congress (LC-USZ62-105139) (Edison).